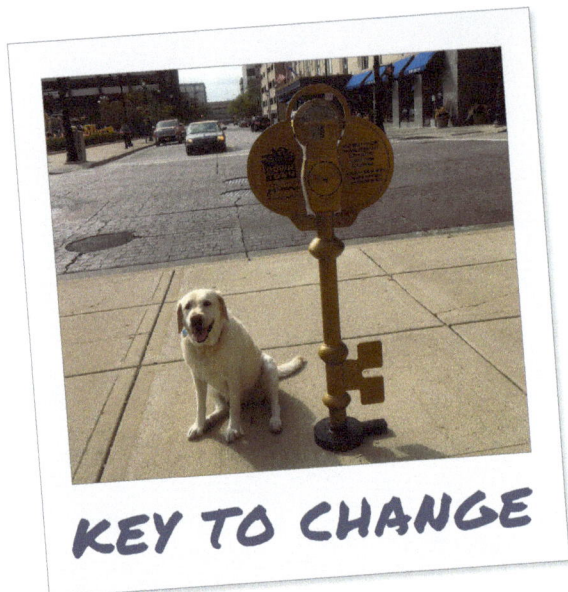

THE ADVENTURES OF BOB: DOWNTOWN MILWAUKEE

Orange Hat Publishing
www.orangehatpublishing.com
Waukesha, WI
414-212-5477

All proceeds from **THE ADVENTURES OF BOB: DOWNTOWN MILWAUKEE** go directly to **Key To Change** in Beth and Joe Weirick's name.

Key To Change is a local campaign in Milwaukee created to assist chronically homeless individuals within our community. 100% of all donations to Key To Change go directly toward housing assistance and support services.

When you find yourself adventuring through Downtown Milwaukee, you too can donate directly to Key To Change when you come across a golden key like Bob did!

For more information:
www.keytochangemke.com

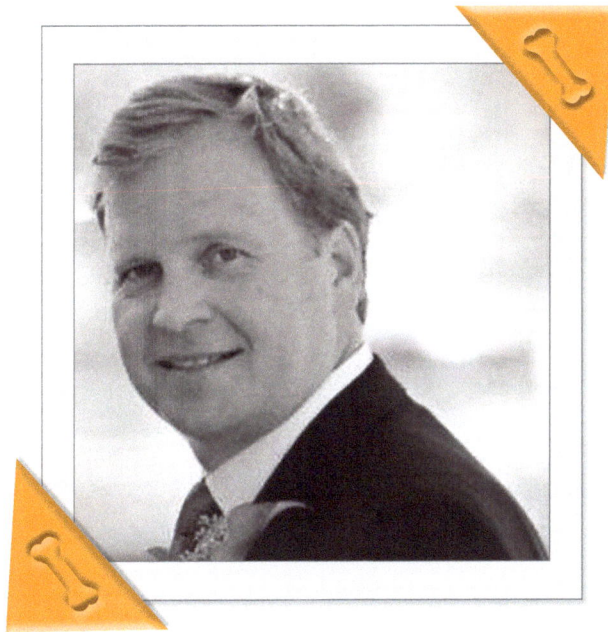

IN LOVING MEMORY OF

Joe Weirick, 1959-2017

DEDICATED TO

My mom and best friend, Beth Weirick, and
the city our family loves to call home: Milwaukee, WI.

Words cannot describe how much my mom, Joe, and the city of Milwaukee have inspired, motivated, and challenged me to be the best I can be.

My clothing line, **#DareToBe**, was created to inspire people to be their absolute best selves and to continue the passion that Joe helped ignite in me.

The legacy that Joe left behind is one that I refuse to let die.

This book is my way of doing my part so that Joe Weirick lives on in all of our hearts, while continuing to breathe life into the city of Milwaukee, the place he lived, loved, and help develop.

Bob, our 11-year-old yellow lab, brings so much joy and love into our home and hearts. I had to share her with the world through her adventures. Yes, her; Bob the girl.

So, this book is for you: A dog lover. An art lover. An adventurer. A city lover. A Milwaukee lover. A friend of Beth and Joe's. A fan of Bob, the girl. Someone that wants to make a difference. Someone that needs a smile. Someone that wants to be inspired. Someone that loves to call Milwaukee home.

Thank you for your purchase of this book and for taking the time to do YOUR part in continuing to carry on the legacy of Joe Weirick.

All proceeds will be donated to **Key To Change**, to help end chronic homelessness, in Beth and Joe Weirick's name. (**www. keytochangemke.com**)

With so much love,

Shawna
DJ Shawna • #DareToBe

> For more information on **#DareToBe** and to purchase **THE ADVENTURES OF BOB: DOWNTOWN MILWAUKEE**
> **www.daretobeclothing.com**
>
> To donate directly to the
> **JOE WEIRICK SCHOLARSHIP FUND**
> **www.joeweirickscholarship.com**

The biggest hug followed by a high-five, with all my love and gratitude, to the team at Graydient Creative. This would not have come to life without all of you. Thank you Danielle, Kristaleen, Sami, and Shawn for your patience, expertise, and talents.

"It is not the critic who counts; not the man who points out how the strong man stumbles, or where the doer of deeds could have done them better. The credit belongs to the man who is actually in the arena, whose face is marred by dust and sweat and blood; who strives valiantly; who errs, who comes short again and again, because there is no effort without error and shortcoming; but who does actually strive to do the deeds; who knows great enthusiasms, the great devotions; who spends himself in a worthy cause; who at the best knows in the end the triumph of high achievement, and who at the worst, if he fails, at least he fails while daring greatly, so that this place shall never be with those cold and timid souls who neither know victory nor defeat."

—THEODORE ROOSEVELT, 1910

INTERMODAL
STATION

I've heard Milwaukee has so much to offer, so I decided I must find out for myself. My unleashed adventure begins at the **Milwaukee Intermodal Station**. Isn't it pretty?

This is the hotel I'm staying at during my visit to Milwaukee. The magnificent **Hilton Milwaukee City Center**!

HILTON MILWAUKEE CITY CENTER

WISCONSIN CENTER

I see a lot of humans head toward the **Wisconsin Center** and the **Milwaukee Women's Center**. Let's see what else is nearby!

My nose knows no lies when it comes to sausages. Just up the road is **Usinger's Famous Sausage**. Can you imagine? It's like a treat factory!

USINGER'S

WISCONSIN AVE

There is so much to do—but where should I start?

Let's ask my friend, **Millie**, **at the Hilton** if she has any recommendations.

This is me with Millie, the hotel concierge. The human is her dad, Rusty.

"Millie, could you tell me what there is to do around here?"

MILLIE AT THE HILTON

MILLIE + ME PLAYING

RUNNING TO MILLIE'S DESK

"Definitely! Here, follow me to my desk," Millie replied excitedly.

"Woooaaahhhh, sweety slow down!" I said, panting. Millie is really fast.

"Take this. It's got lots of fun places to eat, shop, and explore. Humans seem to love them, so I know you will too! You're going to love it here, Bob!"

She gave me a map of downtown Milwaukee.

THANKS, MILLIE!

MAP OF DOWNTOWN MILWAUKEE

EAST TOWN

HISTORIC THIRD WARD

LAKE MICHIGAN

VETERANS PARK

BURNS TRIANGLE PARK

JUNEAU PARK

BMO BRADLEY CENTER

THE MILWAUKEE THEATRE

UW-MILWAUKEE PANTHER ARENA

WISCONSIN CONVENTION CENTER

WAR MEMORIAL CENTER

CALATRAVA ADDITION

MUSEUM DRIVE

U.S. BANK CENTER

SHOPS AT GRAND AVENUE

ZEIDLER PARK

INTERMODAL STATION (AMTRAK /BUS)

UNITED STATES POST OFFICE

HARLEY DAVIDSON MUSEUM

MENOMONEE RIVER

ITALIAN COMMUNITY CENTER

SUMMERFEST GROUNDS

LAKESHORE STATE PARK

H. MAIER FESTIVAL PARK

PIER WISCONSIN DISCOVERY WORLD LAKE DENIS SULLIVAN

Scale
0   500   1000

Milwaukee Map Servic
959 N. Mayfai
Milwaukee, WI 5322
Toll Free 1-800-52
Phone (414) 77
www.mapservi
Copyrig

P.6 P.7 P.8 P.9 P.10 P.16 P. 17–20 P.21 P.22 P.23 P.24 P.25 P.26–27 P.28 P.29 P.30 P.31 P.32–33 P.34–37 P.38 P.39 P.40 P.41

THE SHOPS OF GRAND AVE

Now I begin to explore the city. My first stop is **The Shops of Grand Avenue**. What a cool looking place! They have so many shops AND a food court!

Sounds like my kind of place!

Downtown Milwaukee has a river that goes right through it, like a never-ending water dish! Let's see what we can find along the **Riverwalk**.

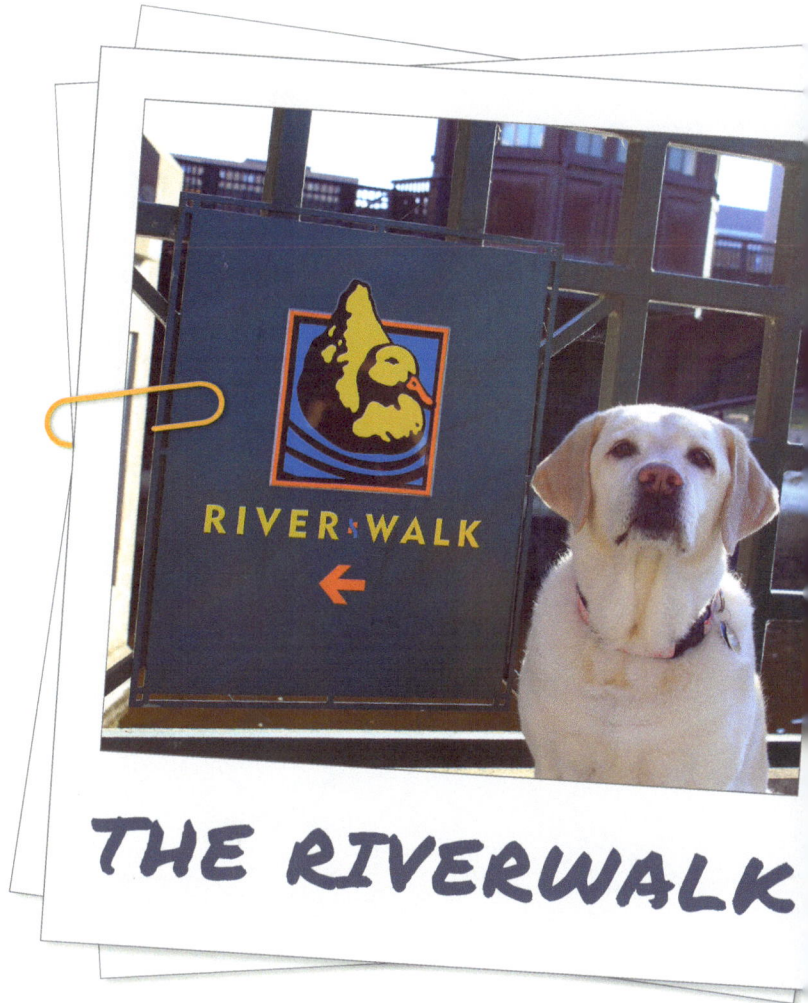

RIVER·WALK

THE RIVERWALK

HEY GERTIE!

"Bark, bark!" A duck! Oh wait, it's just a statue of **Gertie the Duck**.

There is so much to see along **Milwaukee's Riverwalk**, including all kinds of art and architecture.

BRONZE FONZ

That looks like the guy from the TV show "Happy Days." It's the **Bronze Fonz**. Ayyye.

This is nice, but I'm getting kind of hungry. I want a sammich!

ESPIONAGE
.055 km

SAFEHOUSE MILWAUKEE

I smell food coming from this way...

What in the world? A secret spy restaurant? It's called the **SafeHouse**.

INTERNATIONAL EXPORTS, LTD.
779 FRONT ST.
ESTAB. 1866

PERE MARQUETTE PARK

Ahh that was some good grub. Let's see what else is arou—Hurrah! A park! Don't cha know it's in the middle of downtown. It's called **Pere Marquette Park**.

My ball rolled across the bridge to the **Marcus Center for the Performing Arts**.

The **Milwaukee Ballet** performs here. I wonder if they need another dancer?

MARCUS CENTER FOR THE PERFORMING ARTS

INTERCONTINENTAL MILWAUKEE

Oooh, for my ballet debut, I can recommend my friends stay at the **InterContinental Milwaukee**.

Look, it's **Milwaukee's City Hall**.
Woah, that's a tall building.

Maybe I should stop and
tell the mayor how much
I'm enjoying the city.

MILWAUKEE
CITY HALL

CATHEDRAL
SQUARE PARK

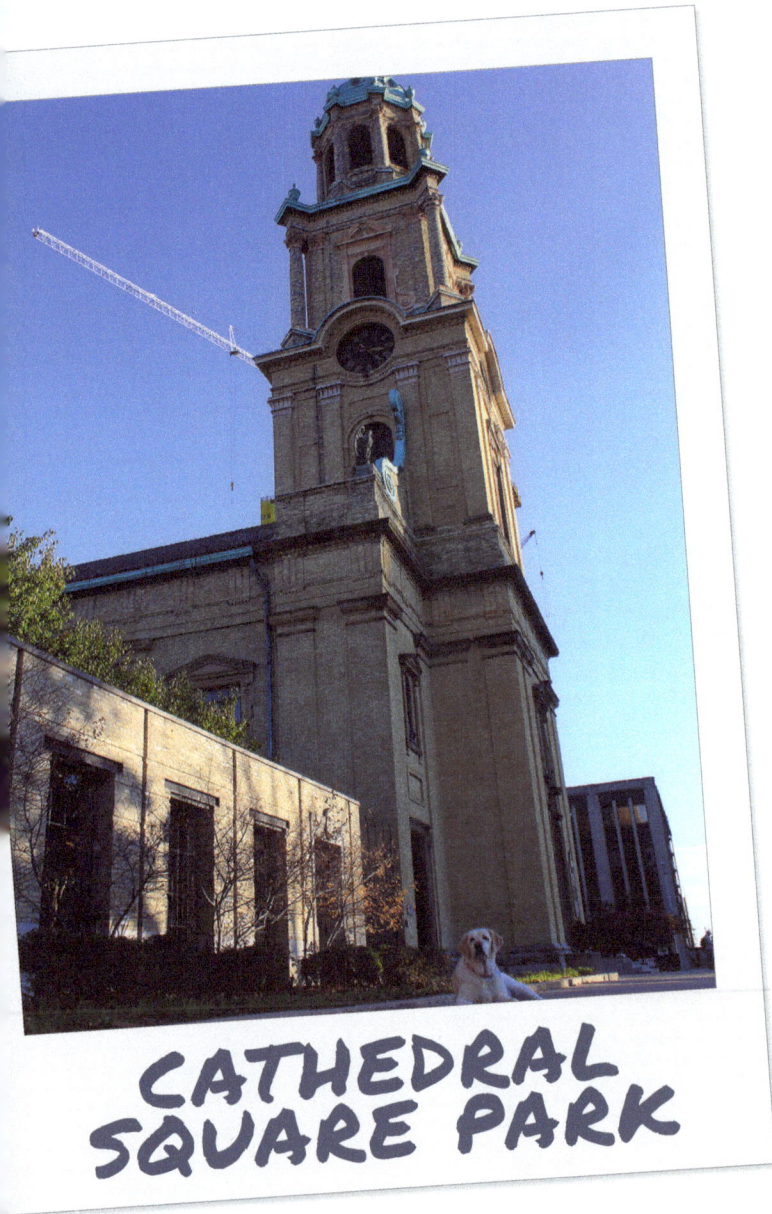

This looks like
Cathedral Square Park.

What a perfect place to
lay in the shade.

Millie told me there were swings over here.... Found them! Now if only they had one for dogs...

YIPEEE!

MAZORCA TACOS

Fudge muffins! I'm hungry again... Mille told me about a yummy taco truck called **Mazorca Tacos** at the end of Water Street.

The map says it's a short walk – good thing walks are my favorite!

The taco place is up the street from my favorite radio station to listen to while I'm here in town—**88Nine Radio Milwaukee**.

I'm going to see if they can spin me up some classic Snoop Dogg.

88NINE RADIO MILWAUKEE

MILWAUKEE
PUBLIC MARKET

I should get a couple of souvenirs while I'm here. The **Milwaukee Public Market** has so many shops and food vendors inside!

My mom would love some soup — if I don't eat it before I get home.

Speaking of home, here is a store called **MilwaukeeHome**. Oh boy, I can't decide which souvenir to get. There are so many options!

MILWAUKEE HOME STORE

UTILITY

BOXES

 Milwaukee has art everywhere.
They even decorated their utility boxes!

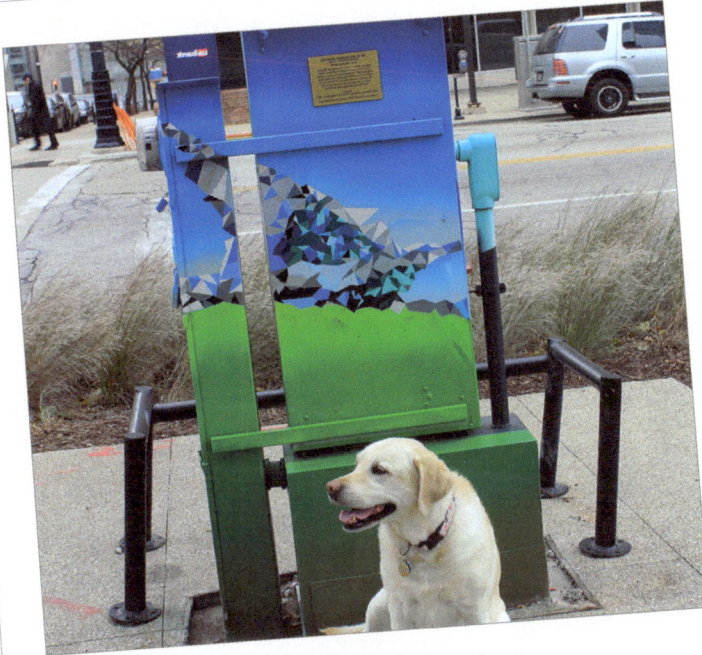

ARTWORK

I'll take a picture and tag the artist, **@MauricioPaints**, on Instagram!

THE PFISTER HOTEL

Here's another hotel. This one is a classic called **The Pfister**.

Before I moved on from **The Pfister Hotel**, I made sure to take a look around. Look how majestic this lobby is!

This is me pretending to be this lion. Pretty good impression, huh?

Of course, they love dogs here, too. Check out the portrait of this guy.

On the top floor they have a lounge called **Blu Milwaukee** with an amazing view of the city.

Look at that lakefront! It's like one long dog park. I think I'll head that way.

BETTY BRINN
CHILDREN'S MUSEUM

Down the street is a cool museum for kids, The **Betty Brinn's Children Museum**. I wonder if they'd let me run around in there...?

What a pretty looking piece of art! And it's huge! This one is called **Sunburst/The Calling**.

SUNBURST / THE CALLING

MILWAUKEE ART MUSEUM

Milwaukee sure does appreciate art. I'll be sure to check out the **Milwaukee Art Museum** during my stay.

Gasp I made it to **Discovery World** which is right along the lakefront.

These are the shores of the glorious **Lake Michigan**. What a lovely sight to see!

DISCOVERY WORLD

Oh boy, this has been a jam-packed, fun-filled day.

I have to start heading back to the **Hilton Milwaukee City Center** and take a nap, even though I wish I could explore all day long.

Oh well, fairness is a goat's butt.

There's so many fun things to do year-round in Milwaukee. I'll have to come back again.

SEE YOU LATER MILWAUKEE!

THANKS TO ALL WHO HELPED TELL MY TALE!

THANK YOU

MILWAUKEE DOWNTOWN
414.220.4700
www.milwaukeedowntown.com
Instagram: @MKEDowntown
Facebook: www.facebook.com/
milwaukeedowntown
Twitter: @MilwDowntown

GRAYDIENT CREATIVE
414.436.0581
www.graydientcreative.com
Instagram: @graydient_creative
Facebook: www.facebook.com/
GraydientCreative
Twitter: @WeAreGraydient

MILWAUKEE INTERMODAL STATION
www.amtrak.com/stations/mke
Instagram: @amtrak
Facebook: www.facebook.com/
ridehiawatha
Twitter: @amtrak

HILTON MILWAUKEE CITY CENTER
414.271.7250
www.hiltonmilwaukee.com
Instagram: @HiltonMilwaukee
Facebook: www.facebook.com/
hiltonmilwaukee
Twitter: @HiltonMilwaukee

WISCONSIN CENTER
414.908.6000
www.wisconsincenter.org
Instagram: @WisconsinCenter
Facebook: www.facebook.com/
WisconsinCenter
Twitter: @WICenterMKE

USINGER'S FAMOUS SAUSAGE
414.276.9105
www.usinger.com
Instagram: @Usingers
Facebook: www.facebook.com/
usingersausage
Twitter: @UsingersSausage

MILLIE AT THE HILTON
www.marcusgiftcards.com/millie
Instagram: @MillieattheHilton

THE SHOPS OF GRAND AVENUE
414.224.0655
grandavenueshops.com
Facebook: www.facebook.com/
TheShopsofGrandAvenue
Twitter: @ShopsofGrandAve

MILWAUKEE RIVERWALK (VISIT MILWAUKEE)
414.273.3950
www.visitmilwaukee.org/riverwalk
Instagram: @VisitMilwaukee
Facebook: www.facebook.com/
visitmilwaukee
Twitter: @VisitMilwaukee

SAFEHOUSE
414.271.2007
www.safe-house.com
Instagram: @SafeHouseMKE
Facebook: www.facebook.com/
SafeHouseMKE
Twitter: @SafeHouseMKE

**PERE MARQUETTE PARK /
CATHEDRAL SQUARE PARK
(MILWAUKEE COUNTY PARKS)**
414.257.7275
county.milwaukee.gov/Parks
Instagram: @MKECountyParks
Facebook: www.facebook.com/
MilwaukeeCountyParks
Twitter: @CountyParks

**MARCUS CENTER FOR
THE PERFORMING ARTS**
414.273.7206
www.marcuscenter.org
Instagram: @Marcus.Center
Facebook: www.facebook.com/
MarcusCenter.org
Twitter: @MarcusCenter

**INTERCONTINENTAL
MILWAUKEE**
414.276.8686
www.intercontinentalmilwaukee.
com
Facebook: www.facebook.com/
InterContinentalMilwaukee
Twitter: @InterConMKE

MILWAUKEE CITY HALL
city.milwaukee.gov/home
Twitter: @CityOfMilwaukee

MAZORCA TACOS
414.810.6603
Instagram: @MazorcaMKE
Facebook: www.facebook.com/
mazorcamke

88NINE RADIO MILWAUKEE
414.892.8900
radiomilwaukee.org
Instagram: @RadioMilwaukee
Facebook: www.facebook.
com/88nine
Twitter: @RadioMilwaukee

MILWAUKEE PUBLIC MARKET
414.336.1111
www.milwaukeepublicmarket.org
Instagram: @
MilwaukeePublicMarket
Facebook: www.facebook.com/
MilwaukeePublicMarket
Twitter: @MKEPublicMarket

MILWAUKEE HOME
414.731.5339
www.mkehome.com
Instagram: @MilwaukeeHome
Facebook: www.facebook.com/
MKEHome
Twitter: @Milwaukee_Home

MAURICIO RAMIREZ
mauriciopaints.com
Instagram: @MauricioPaints
Facebook: www.facebook.com/
MauricioRamirezArt
Twitter: @MauricioPaints

THE PFISTER HOTEL
414.273.8222
www.thepfisterhotel.com
Instagram: @ThePfisterHotel
Facebook: www.facebook.com/
thePfisterHotel
Twitter: @PfisterHotel

**BETTY BRINN CHILDREN'S
MUSEUM**
414.390.5437
www.bbcmkids.org
Instagram: @
BettyBrinnChildrensMuseum
Facebook: www.facebook.com/
bettybrinn
Twitter: @BBCMMilwaukee

**"THE CALLING" SCULPTURE,
AKA "SUNBURST", 1981–1982**
by Mark di Suvero
www.spacetimecc.com

MILWAUKEE ART MUSEUM
414.224.3200
mam.org
Instagram: @MilwaukeeArt
Facebook: www.facebook.com/
milwaukeeart
Twitter: @MilwaukeeArt

DISCOVERY WORLD
414.765.9966
www.discoveryworld.org
Instagram: @DiscoveryWorldMKE
Facebook: www.facebook.com/
DiscoveryWorldMKE
Twitter: @DiscoveryWorld

www.ingramcontent.com/pod-product-compliance
Lightning Source LLC
Chambersburg PA
CBHW041958100426
42813CB00019B/2920